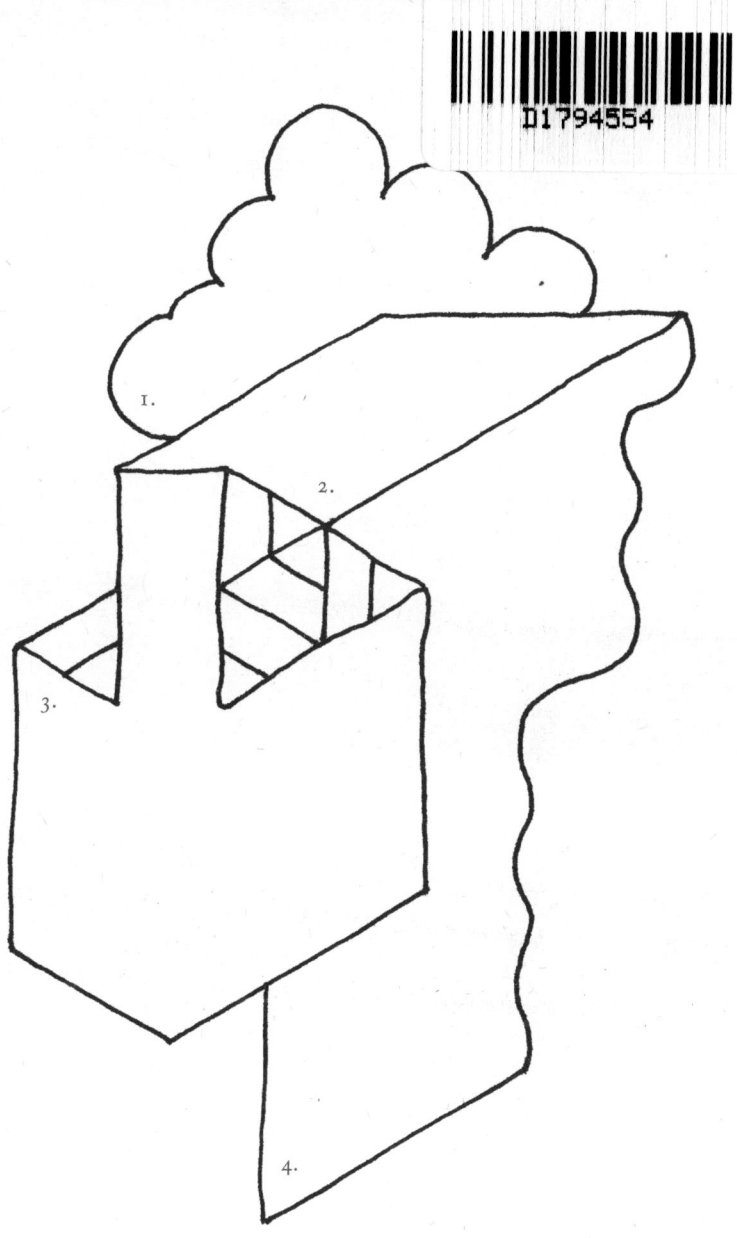

1. Month
2. This manual belongs to
3. This month, I intend
4. Theme of this month

Monthly Manifestation Manual

A 31-DAY GUIDED JOURNAL FOR CREATING YOUR BEST LIFE

Jessica Mullen
Kelly Cree

Monthly Manifestation Manual:
A 31-Day Guided Journal for Creating Your Best Life
© Jessica Mullen and Kelly Cree 2023

ISBN 9781648412257
This is Microcosm #744
First Published, 2012
Second Edition, First Published June 13, 2023
This edition © Microcosm Publishing, 2023

Microcosm Publishing
2752 N Williams Ave
Portland, OR 97227
(503)799-2698

OTHER ZINES, BOOKS, STICKERS, PATCHES, PINS, POSTERS, T-SHIRTS, DVDS, & MORE:
WWW.MICROCOSM.PUB

To join the ranks of high-class stores that feature Microcosm titles, talk to your rep: In the U.S. **Como** (Atlantic), **Abraham** (Midwest), **Bob Barnett** (Texas/Louisiana/Oklahoma), **imprint group** (Pacific), **Turnaround** (Europe,) **UTP/Manda** (Canada), **New South** (Australia/New Zealand), **GPS** in Asia, Africa, India, South America, and other countries, or **FAIRE** in the gift trade.

Did you know that you can buy our books directly from us at sliding scale rates? Support a small, independent publisher and pay less than Amazon's price at **www.Microcosm.Pub**

This book is dedicated to our soldiers of light. Thank you for playing.

We thank Abraham-Hicks, Alan Watts, Osho, Eckhart Tolle, Wayne Dyer, Deepak Chopra, Kamal Ravikant, Louise Hay, Rumi, Danielle Laporte, and Drunvalo Melchizedek for their
wisdom and willingness to share.

Eternal gratitude to Fede, Ryan, Tracy, Jenny, Stephen, Karen, Sheima, Jimmy, Jamar, Dee Dee, Betty, Magen, Sam, Tina, Cory, Boni, Connie, Jennifer, Nate, Ethan, Kenth, our families, and each and every SoLDier for inspiring and encouraging us along the way.

To every friend who passed through the
Rave Cave and filled out one of our worksheets, thank you.

Dear friend,

This *Monthly Manifestation Manual* is a comprehensive workbook for designing your life. Much like a monthly planner, it is intended to help you maintain focus on the life of your dreams.

For each day of a 31-day month, *MMM* provides a repeating template for summarizing intentions, wishes, and mantras. This daily practice is a constant reminder of your power as a creator and helps you gather momentum as you carve out the riverbeds of new thought patterns.

Following each daily practice page is a unique exercise carefully constructed to help you define your desires, practice feeling the way you want to feel, and allow more abundance and joy into your life. With each day comes a new perspective, a new idea, and a new way of understanding what you already know.

Your attention is your most valuable resource. What you focus on expands. This book will help you place your focus on what you want and what you want more of. This powerful book of spells has the ability to bring you anything you want. The only limit is your imagination.

Believe in your own magick and take your personal power to the next level. If you ever feel lost or don't know what to do, just meditate on love and the rest will flow. Happy conscious creating!

Love,
Kelly Cree and Jessica Mullen
SCHOOLOFLIFEDESIGN.COM

Fill out the calendar to the right according to when you start this manual so you can keep track of important dates, patterns, and manifestations in your life design practice.

Have a Great Day!

When you practice telling the universe, "Yes, please! More, please!" every day, you gather momentum. The most important aspect, though, is the practice. Conscious creation is just like a team sport: the more regularly you practice, the more skilled you become. Use the template at the right as it is repeated throughout the manual to practice your magick every day, and you will notice your powers expand.

1. Write the date or name your day something special or silly.

2. What did you dream about last night? What are your current life dreams?

3. Choose a theme for the day that will help you focus your attention.

4. Often, when we feel responsible for completing a task, it becomes impossible to check off of a to-do list. When you stop caring about if something gets done, your attention is no longer creating the reality of, "This thing isn't done!" This becomes your list of things to not give a fuck about.

5. What are your intentions for the day? Keep them with you in all moments.

6. Choose a mental code to return to whenever you find your thoughts wandering, or when you notice a dip in your mood. It will keep your focus on the divine energy within you, instead of on the usual worries and unease you may experience while thinking.

7. Use the list of example emotions below to help decide how you want to feel.

JOY	LOVE	HAPPINESS
EUPHORIA	EXHILARATION	BELIEF
FLOW	KNOWING	OPTIMISM
INSPIRATION	PASSION	HOPE
APPRECIATION	EXCITEMENT	CONTENTMENT
EMPOWERMENT	ENTHUSIASM	RELIEF
FREEDOM	EAGERNESS	CONFIDENCE

8. List the best parts of your day as they happen. This works like a magickal grocery list: whatever you write down, you're asking for more of.

9. Make a wish, because when you ask, it is given!

10. Finally, take a brief moment to think about how you want to feel the next morning. When you take the time to plan how you want to feel, the feeling comes on its own without you having to try.

1. Date
2. Dreams
3. Today's theme
4. To ~~do~~ not give a fuck about
5. Intentions
6. Today's mantra/affirmation
7. I want to feel
8. Best parts of my day
9. Make a wish
10. Tomorrow I will wake up feeling

Best Case Scenarios

Often, we dread the worst case scenario and forget to ask ourselves the best that can happen. As you begin your magickal journey this month, visualize the best possible outcome for each entry on the next page. Then celebrate! The universe wants that version for you and is conspiring to make it happen.

Identifying the best you can imagine for yourself helps you pulse the signal of having what you want, right now. When you send a signal, the universe reflects that signal. When you feel as if you have something, the universe shows you more evidence. As you imagine each best possible outcome, feel what it would feel like if it came true. In the moment that you feel as if you have it, you already do.

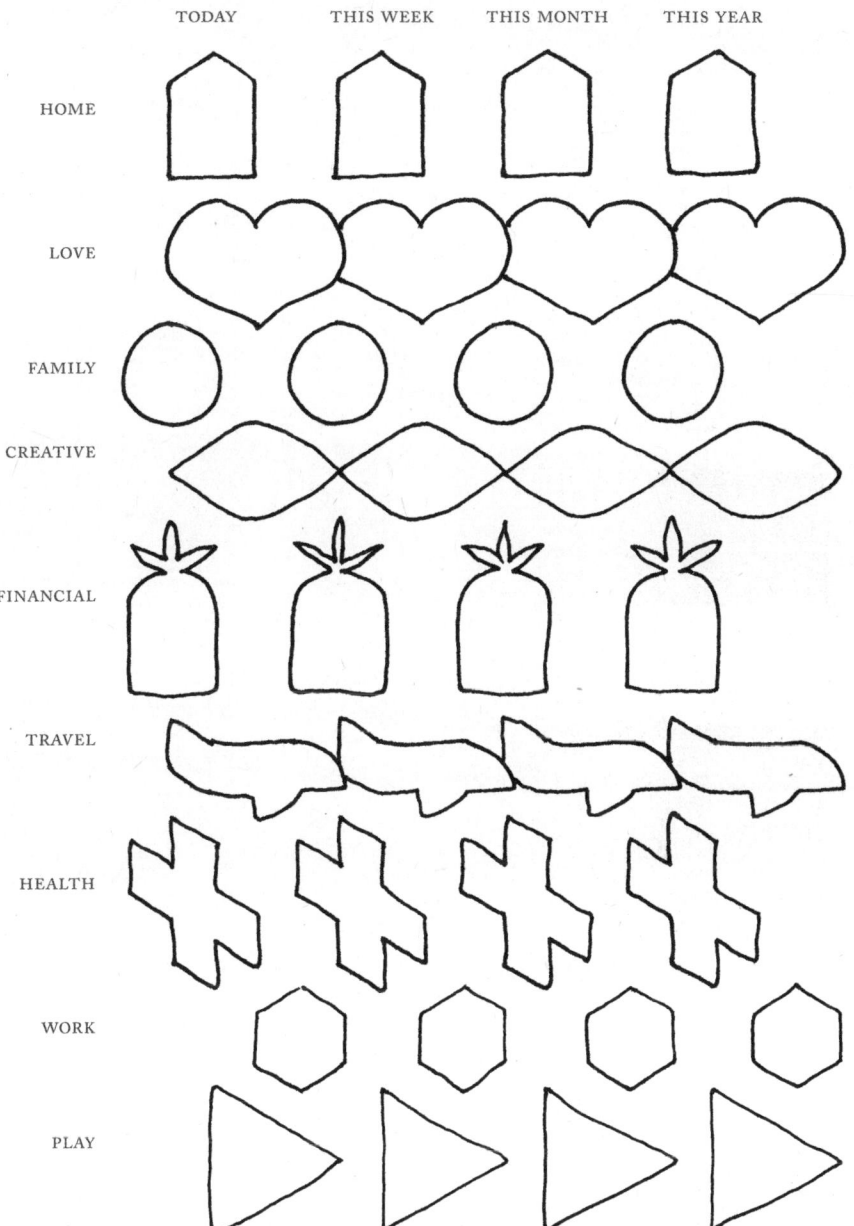

1. Date
2. Dreams
3. Today's theme
4. To do not give a fuck about
5. Intentions
6. Today's mantra/affirmation
7. I want to feel
8. Best parts of my day
9. Make a wish
10. Tomorrow I will wake up feeling

Upward Spiral

Now that you've imagined the best possible outcomes for the magickal month to come, the easiest way to maintain a sense of positive focus and expectation is with gratitude.

When you worry or stress, you pinch off the flow of well-being. When you are acutely aware of the gifts in every moment, you openly welcome the flow to flow through you. When the flow is flowing through you, life is able to more quickly manifest your desires.

Start this *Upward Spiral* at the center with tiny things for which you can feel gratitude. Maybe the hot cup of coffee you had this morning or the fact that you have running water and a pot to piss in. Explore the minutiae of your life to discover what you already have that you can be grateful for. As you start to look for them, you will notice that more and more ideas flood to your mind. There is so much to be grateful for!

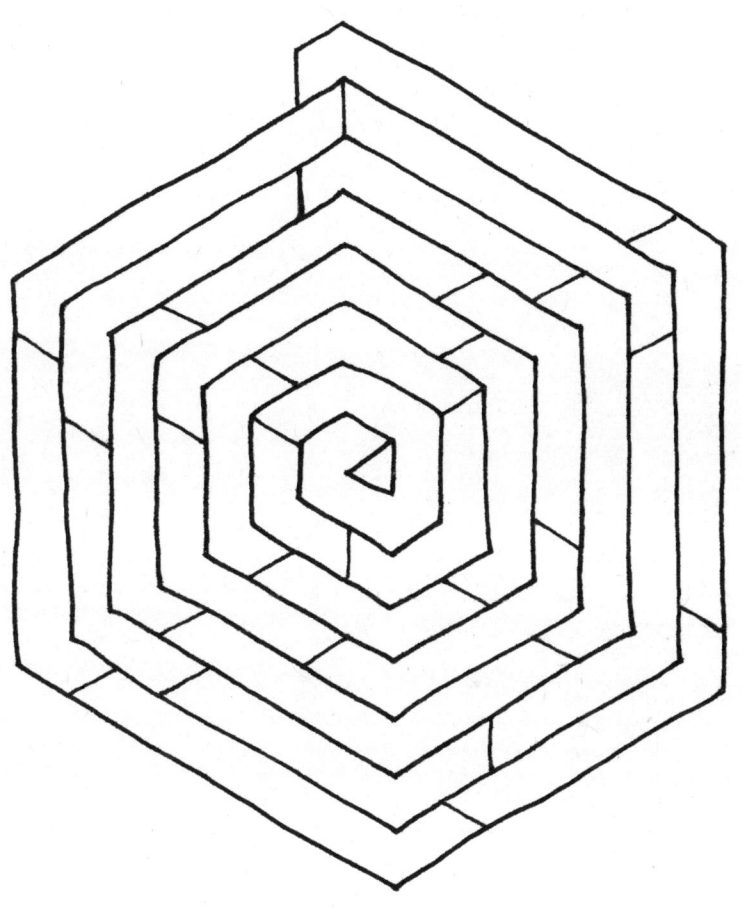

1. Date
2. Dreams
3. Today's theme
4. To ~~do~~ not give a fuck about
5. Intentions
6. Today's mantra/affirmation
7. I want to feel
8. Best parts of my day
9. Make a wish
10. Tomorrow I will wake up feeling

What Do I Want?

This exercise is designed to help you figure out what you want. What you want will always change, by the day, the hour, or the minute. And once you get what you want, you'll want something else. Doing this worksheet will keep you busy identifying fresh desires based on the prompts given. You can stop thinking about your old, stale desires so they can finally manifest.

Once you figure out what you want, you don't have to set goals or timelines or start chipping away at to-do lists. You only have to forget about your desire by finding a way to feel good without it. When you ask, it is given; just trust that the universe is on the case. Keep coming up with fresh desires to distract yourself from the old ones and watch as the old desires manifest faster and faster into your experience.

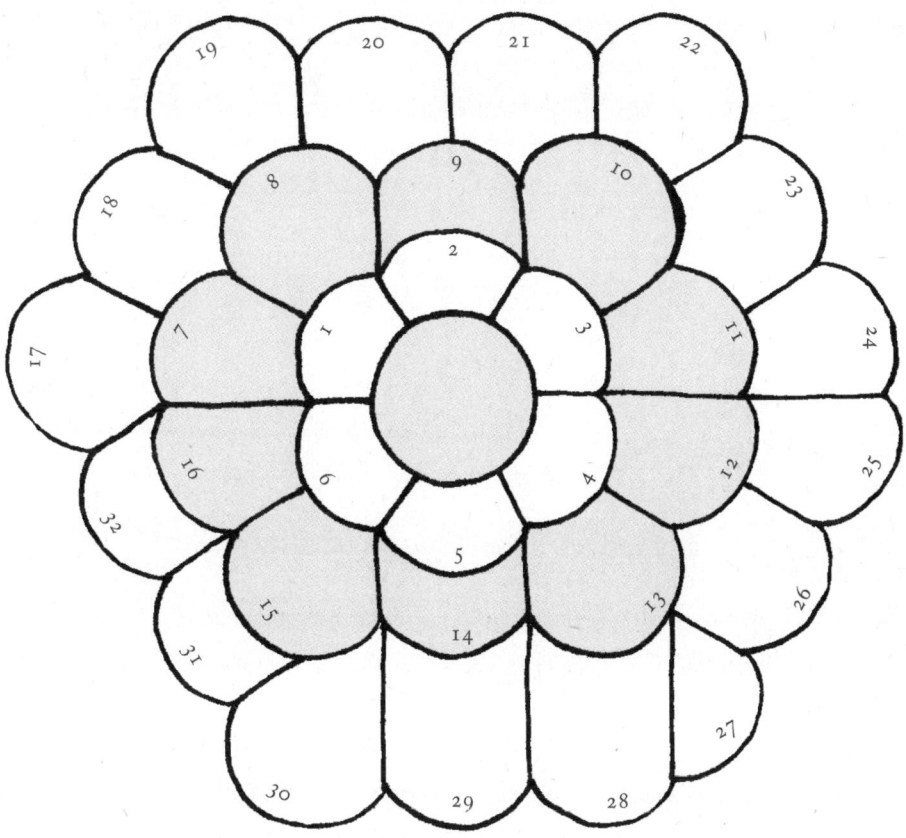

WHAT I WANT TO
1. See 2. Touch 3. Hear
4. Smell 5. Taste 6. Think

HOW I WANT TO FEEL ABOUT MY
7. Body 8. Finances 9. Friends
10. Family 11. Work 12. Thoughts
13. Home 14. Life

DOING
15. What I want to do
16. Where 17. With whom 18. Why

CREATING
19. What I want to create
20. Where 21. With whom 22. Why

WHAT / WHY
23. What or whom I want to be
24. Why I want to be that

25. Where I want to be
26. Why I want to be there

27. What I want for my home
28. Why I want that for my home

29. What I want for my body
30. Why I want that for my body

31. Objects I would like to own
32. Why I want to own these objects

1. Date
2. Dreams
3. Today's theme
4. To ~~do~~ not give a fuck about
5. Intentions
6. Today's mantra/affirmation
7. I want to feel
8. Best parts of my day
9. Make a wish
10. Tomorrow I will wake up feeling

Universal Order Form

This order-number system is a way to trick your mind into practicing the feeling of belief that your wish is actually being granted. Say you ask for a milkshake, and you pick the number 33. An hour goes by and the next time you look at the clock, it says 4:33. A quiver of excitement goes up your spine, as you remember, "My order number is 33!" That feeling is the delicious sensation of trust in the universe, the knowing that what you want is coming and you don't have to lift a finger.

Write your request in the space on the right. Then choose an order number for your item. Make it a number that means something to you, so you'll feel good when you see it. The universe will show you this number when your order is shipped. Thank you for trusting the universe!

1. Date
2. Dreams
3. Today's theme
4. To do not give a fuck about
5. Intentions
6. Today's mantra/affirmation
7. I want to feel
8. Best parts of my day
9. Make a wish
10. Tomorrow I will wake up feeling

⟨5⟩
What's Working?

You can always find something that's going well.
The more you place your attention on what's working, the more evidence you'll notice. What are a few things that you appreciate about various aspects of your life? Focus on those and nothing else, and the parts that aren't working will disappear.

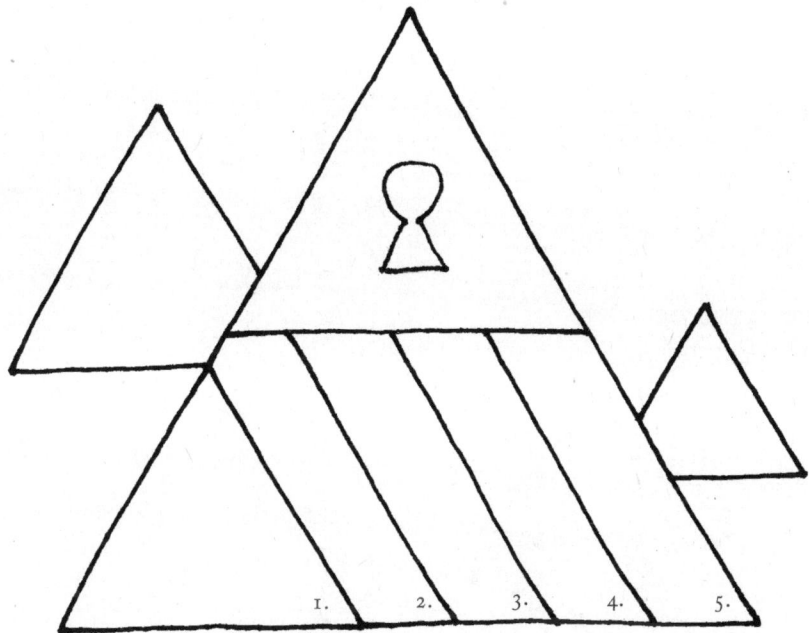

1. Health
2. Work
3. Creative
4. Home
5. Relationships

1. Date
2. Dreams
3. Today's theme
4. To ~~do~~ not give a fuck about
5. Intentions
6. Today's mantra/affirmation
7. I want to feel
8. Best parts of my day
9. Make a wish
10. Tomorrow I will wake up feeling

Success of Another

Do you ever find yourself feeling jealous or resentful of others' success? The mind has a tendency to think, "But why don't I have that?!" When we release the judgment of the mind, however, we realize that the success of others is a reflection of our own alignment with source.

Celebrate success wherever you see it and you will attract more and become more aware of your own accomplishments.

1. Write the name of someone who has experienced success.
2. Write their success story.

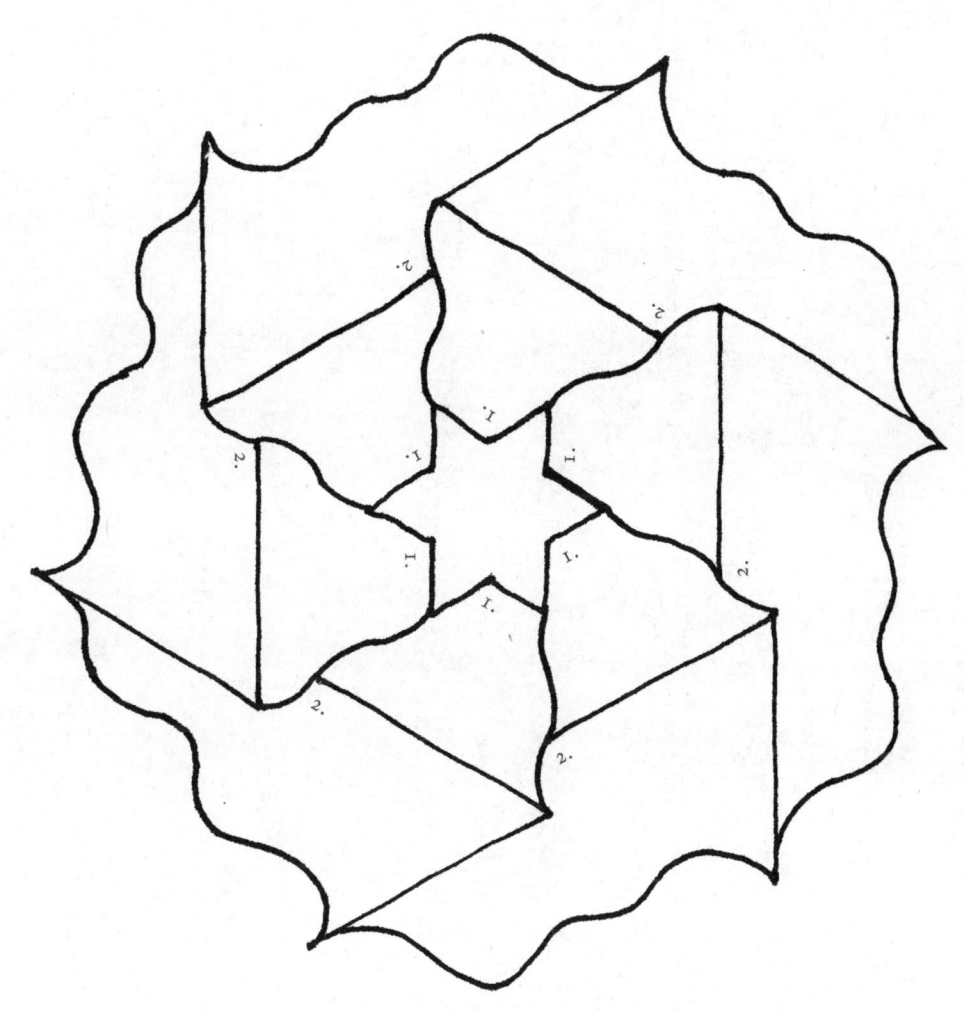

1. Date
2. Dreams
3. Today's theme
4. To do not give a fuck about
5. Intentions
6. Today's mantra/affirmation
7. I want to feel
8. Best parts of my day
9. Make a wish
10. Tomorrow I will wake up feeling

Scavenger Hunt

When you look for something, you find more of it.
When you get your mind in the practice of looking for what you want,
you'll notice that you see it more frequently.

Look for evidence in your life of each of the items on the right and
describe it in the space provided.

Notice how when you look for something, you see it more and more?
That principle can be applied to any aspect of your life.

1. Hidden Treasure
2. Magick
3. Synchronicity
4. Hilarity
5. Well Being
6. Health
7. Love
8. Alien Activity
9. Effortlessness

1. Date
2. Dreams
3. Today's theme
4. To ~~do~~ not give a fuck about
5. Intentions
6. Today's mantra/affirmation
7. I want to feel
8. Best parts of my day
9. Make a wish
10. Tomorrow I will wake up feeling

Greatest Accomplishments

Sometimes we get so caught up thinking about how far we have to go that we forget to celebrate how far we've come. No matter how far you have left to go, you can always think of something you've accomplished in the last day, month, year, or lifetime. Even if it's something small, focusing on what you've accomplished keeps you optimistic.

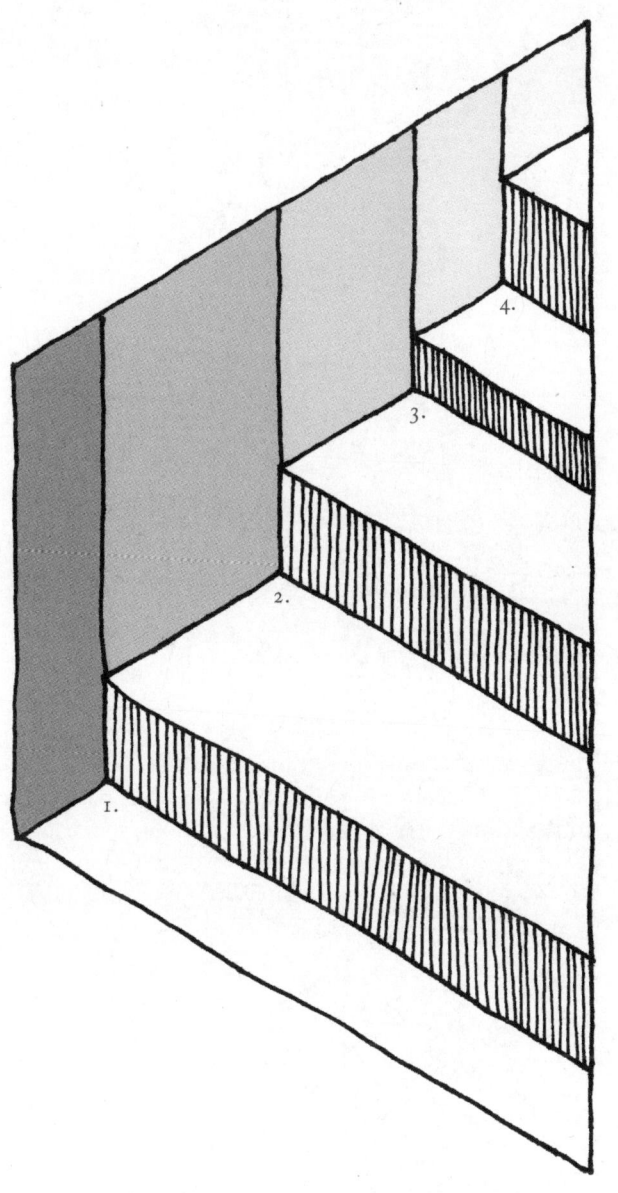

1. Today
2. This month
3. This year
4. Lifetime

1. Date
2. Dreams
3. Today's theme
4. To do not give a fuck about
5. Intentions
6. Today's mantra/affirmation
7. I want to feel
8. Best parts of my day
9. Make a wish
10. Tomorrow I will wake up feeling

6 Wishes

Quick, make six wishes! Write each desire in a candle on the right, then relax and know that your wish is on its way. When you ask, it is given! It might look different than you expected when it comes, but when you let your wish go and trust that it's coming, it is guaranteed to manifest.

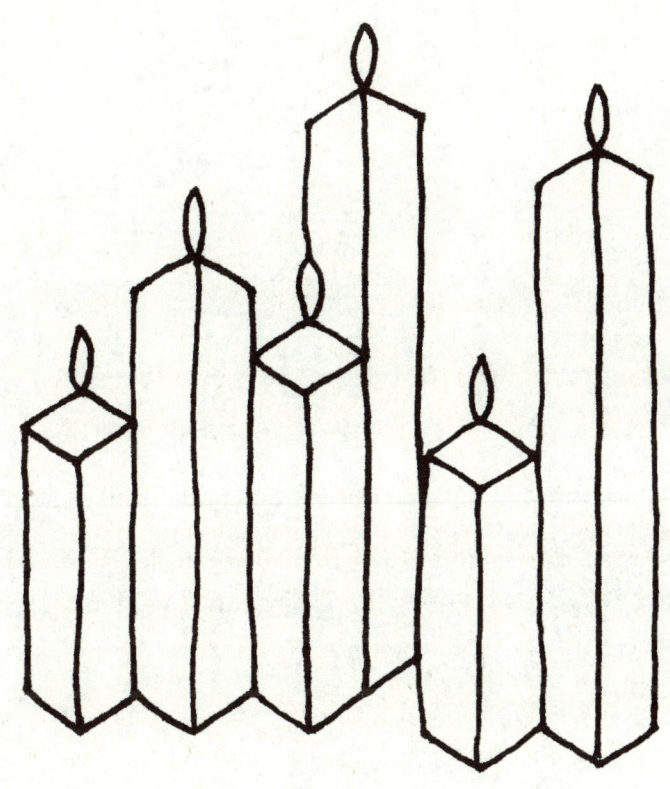

1. Date
2. Dreams
3. Today's theme
4. To ~~do~~ not give a fuck about
5. Intentions
6. Today's mantra/affirmation
7. I want to feel
8. Best parts of my day
9. Make a wish
10. Tomorrow I will wake up feeling

Counting

"When a thought subsides, you experience a discontinuity in the mental stream—a gap of 'no-mind.' When these gaps occur, you feel a certain stillness and peace inside you."

ECKHART TOLLE

There's nothing wrong with thinking, but most of us have some thought patterns we wouldn't mind dropping. Focusing on silent counting creates a space in your mind where you can rest.

When you stop thinking resistant thoughts, your mood improves. When your mood improves, the solutions come to you.

Count each shape in the image on the right. Color or mark each one as you go. Focus all of your attention on the numbers, instead of thinking about things in the background.

You will feel a sense of peace overcome you. You will know truths that you cannot define. You will know these truths without ever having to "learn" them.

This feeling is the flow. You allow it when you release resistant thoughts. Through all your seeking, you will never find it; it must find you.

1. Date
2. Dreams
3. Today's theme
4. To ~~do~~ not give a fuck about
5. Intentions
6. Today's mantra/affirmation
7. I want to feel
8. Best parts of my day
9. Make a wish
10. Tomorrow I will wake up feeling

Wouldn't It Be Nice?

Sometimes we can get so stuck on worrying about what we don't want to happen, it can be hard to even imagine a different scenario. Thought patterns gather momentum, and when you've been thinking one for a long time, imagining a more positive outcome can be frustrating.

But wouldn't it be nice if it all worked out? You don't even have to believe that it will, but wouldn't it be nice if it did?

Wouldn't it be so grand?

Imagine your desires from a more playful point of view.
You don't *need* this outcome, but wouldn't it be nice? Especially those old, stale desires—those things you've been wanting forever—your happiness isn't as dependent on them as you think.
Sure, it would be nice, but it's not necessary.

Write your wishes in the space provided on the next page, send them over the rainbow, and be okay with them never coming true.

But it sure will be nice when they do.

1. Date
2. Dreams
3. Today's theme
4. To ~~do~~ not give a fuck about
5. Intentions
6. Today's mantra/affirmation
7. I want to feel
8. Best parts of my day
9. Make a wish
10. Tomorrow I will wake up feeling

Funny HaHa

"Some people list the things they are grateful for. This is a good list to do. But I try to also list the things around me that are funny. The things that are more than funny. The things that are ludicrous."

JAMES ALTUCHER

Gratitude lists are quite effective at lifting your mood, but they can become monotonous. When you're not feeling great, a gratitude list can seem like a list of things that make you feel guilty, or things that you feel obligated to feel grateful for because you're afraid of losing them.

At times like these, we like to make a different kind of list—one that's more fun and playful. When you look for the things that are funny in your life, you turn your attention toward something else. You're not looking at what you do or don't have, you're just looking to laugh. You release. When you laugh, you shake up all that stagnant energy.

Don't look for things to be grateful for today, just look for things that make you chuckle. Things that make you cackle. Things that bowl you over. Ludicrous things you never could have imagined! Let the humor of life lift you up to see it's really not serious.

1. Things that are funny
2. Things that are more than funny
3. Things that are ludicrous

1. Date
2. Dreams
3. Today's theme
4. To do not give a fuck about
5. Intentions
6. Today's mantra/affirmation
7. I want to feel
8. Best parts of my day
9. Make a wish
10. Tomorrow I will wake up feeling

⟨13⟩
Positive Aspects

Do you have a co-worker or neighbor that drives you crazy? Maybe a situation in your life that you can't stop stressing about or can't let go? Try writing a list of positive aspects about that element of your reality in the web on the right.

Life is your dream. What you see more of in your dream is up to you. Write about what you want to see or even how this trying situation could possibly be beneficial in the end.

When this situation crosses your mind and you're tempted to send a signal of hate, fear, or resentment, picture your web of positive aspects and allow the negative ones to slip down the spiders and out of your reality.

POSITIVE ASPECTS OF
_____

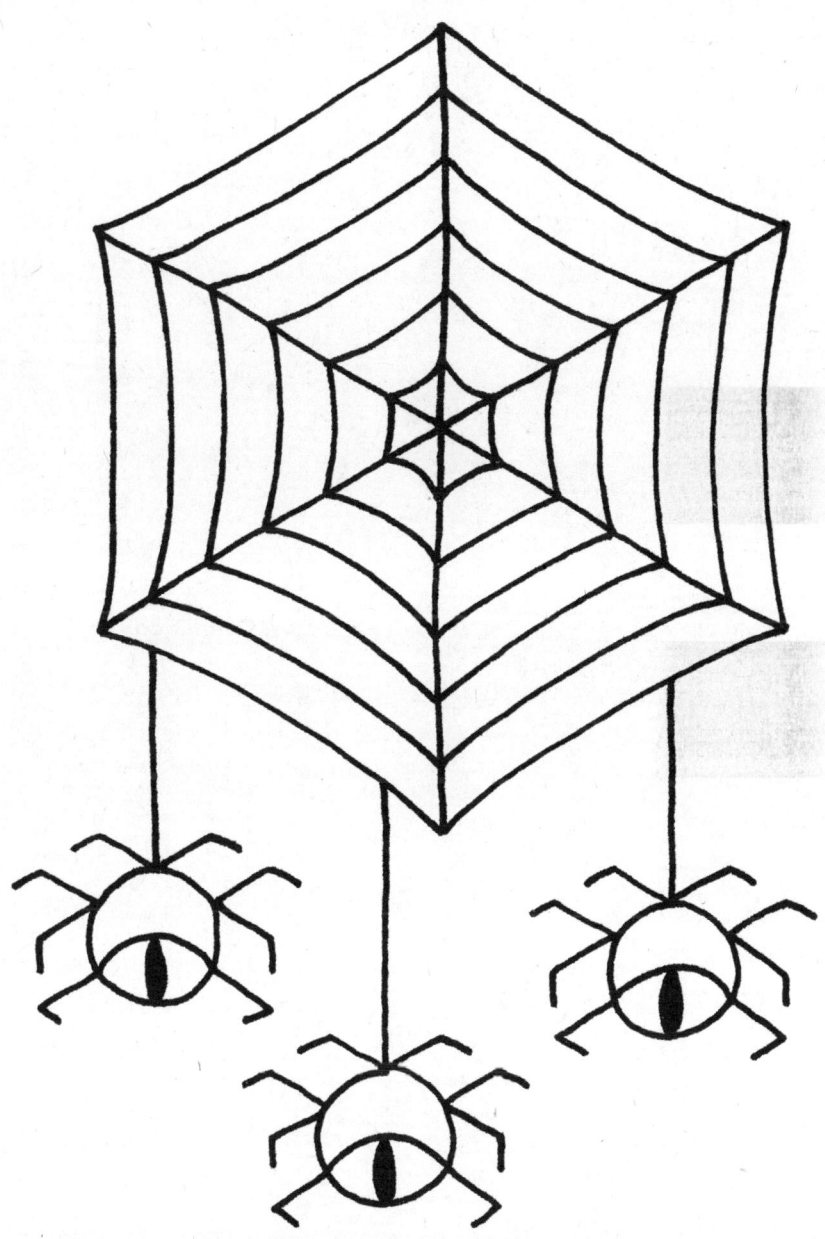

1. Date
2. Dreams
3. Today's theme
4. To ~~do~~ not give a fuck about
5. Intentions
6. Today's mantra/affirmation
7. I want to feel
8. Best parts of my day
9. Make a wish
10. Tomorrow I will wake up feeling

What's Your Solution?

Life exists in waves. Every aspect of life has an opposite, and that is why we are able to experience both. Without one, there cannot be the other. With every problem exists a solution. Awareness of the solution is a matter of focus. When we are overcome by a problem, it can be difficult to see a solution. It can be difficult to even believe in its existence.

Sometimes, we have to just stop looking for the solution. But at the same time, stop looking at the problem. Feel for the feeling you prefer to feel, and life will fill in the rest.

1. Write down your problem in the space indicated. How does your problem make you feel? Circle the emotion in the list above the PROBLEM section.

2. Now find the opposite emotion in the list on the right and circle it. That is the feeling that your problem is causing you to ask for. List 6 things that make you feel that emotion in the space labeled LIST.

3. **Now forget about your problem. Forget about the solution.** The SOLUTION area of the pyramid is intentionally left blank to leave space for it to arise. Focus not on the solution to your problem, but on the feeling you'll feel when it is resolved.

If you find yourself thinking about the problem, say to yourself, "I've decided to feel good about that. It's working itself out." Then remember an item on your list and feel your desired feeling. When you forget the problem, the solution will present itself.

BOREDOM	HOPEFULNESS
PESSIMISM	OPTIMISM
FRUSTRATION, ANNOYANCE	POSITIVE EXPECTATION, BELIEF
OVERWHELMENT, DISAPPOINTMENT	SATISFACTION
DOUBT, WORRY, BLAME	ENTHUSIASM, EAGERNESS
DISCOURAGEMENT	HAPPINESS
ANGER, REVENGE	PASSION
HATE, JEALOUSY	JOY, APPRECIATION, LOVE
INSECURITY, GUILT, UNWORTHINESS	KNOWING, FREEDOM
FEAR, DEPRESSION, DESPAIR	ECSTASY

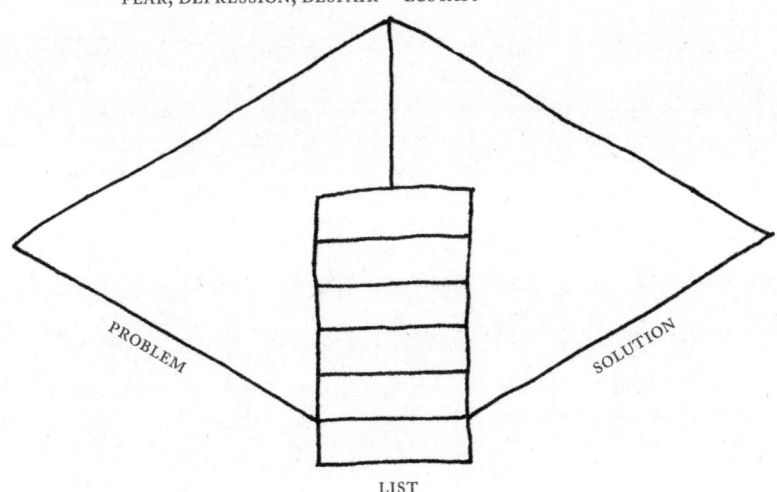

1. Date
2. Dreams
3. Today's theme
4. To ~~do~~ not give a fuck about
5. Intentions
6. Today's mantra/affirmation
7. I want to feel
8. Best parts of my day
9. Make a wish
10. Tomorrow I will wake up feeling

◁15▷

Status Meeting

Whether your projects are self-initiated or you work for someone else, continuing to focus on what's working is the best way to get more.

Even though we know deep down that the universe is growing our business or that millions are clamoring to pay for our work, sometimes the distractions of life can lead the mind down a path of doubt.

Consistently sending a clear, strong signal of positive expectation for the outcome we desire is the best way to allow the universe to do its work through us.

Use the dossier on the next page to have a *Status Meeting* with yourself. Use the prompts to help you tune yourself to how you want to feel about your work. When you embody the feeling of success, you're already there!

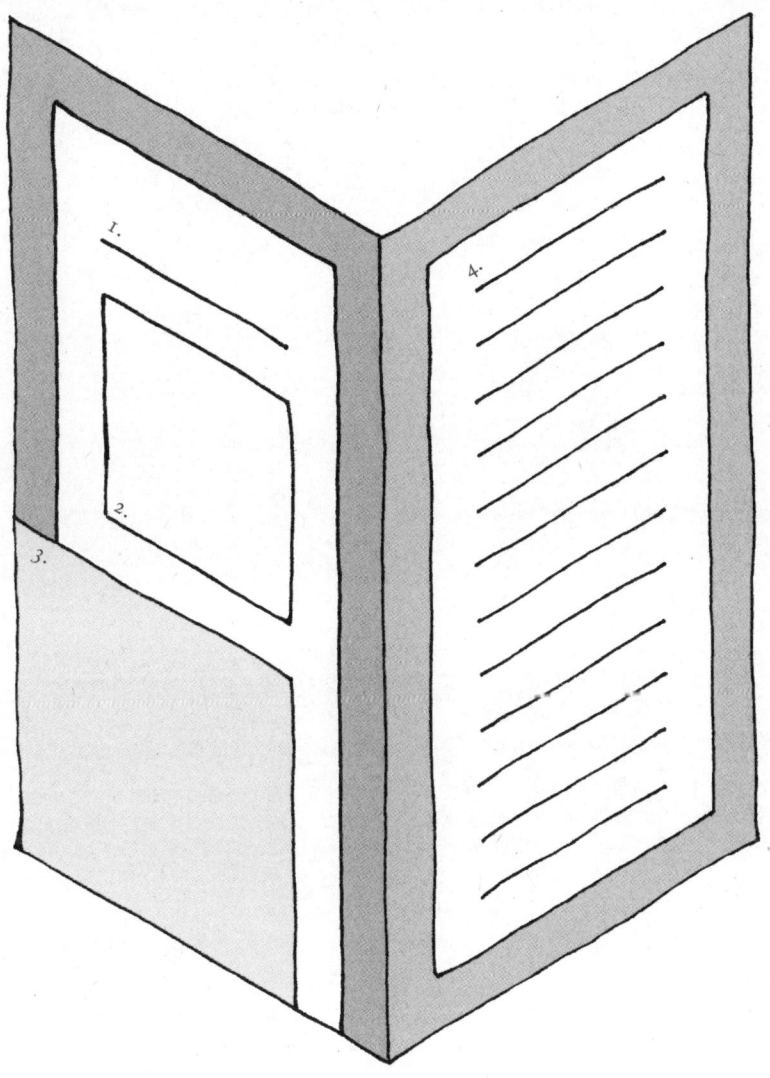

1. How do you want to feel about your work?
2. When do you feel successful?
3. What is one step you can take in the direction of the flow?
4. Write a list of what is going well.

1. Date
2. Dreams
3. Today's theme
4. To do not give a fuck about
5. Intentions
6. Today's mantra/affirmation
7. I want to feel
8. Best parts of my day
9. Make a wish
10. Tomorrow I will wake up feeling

16. The Award Goes To

Name a person, place or thing for each award below. It's fun to notice elements of your life that stand out. What players in your reality deserve a gold star? Praise the aspects of your universe that shine and they will show you more facets of their excellence.

~

1. Best Idea
2. Most Valuable Player
3. You Are My Sunshine
4. Funniest
5. Up and Coming

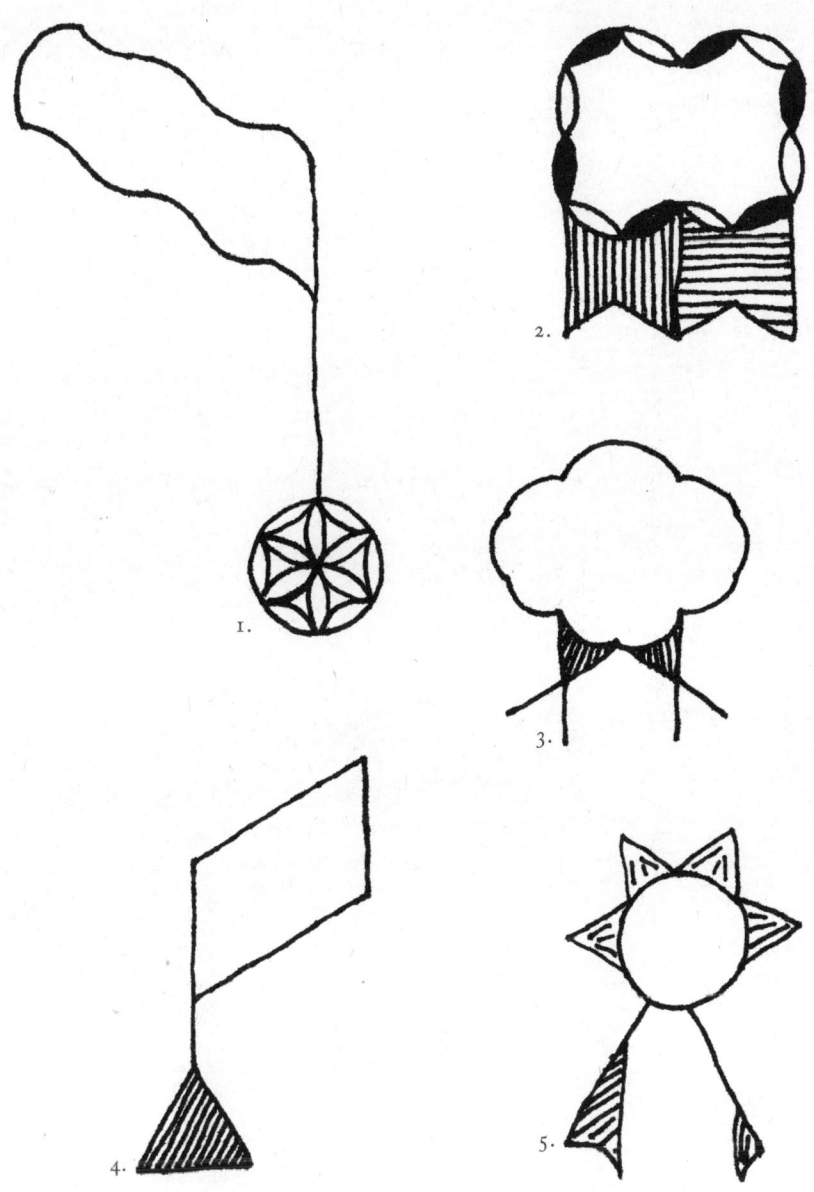

1. Date
2. Dreams
3. Today's theme
4. To ~~do~~ not give a fuck about
5. Intentions
6. Today's mantra/affirmation
7. I want to feel
8. Best parts of my day
9. Make a wish
10. Tomorrow I will wake up feeling

17

I Want to Feel Better

This flow-chart emulates a software program. The mind, like a computer, likes to run in loops. When you get caught in a thought-loop, it can be difficult to break that cycle and form a new thought. If you want your mind software to run a different program, you have to write it.

The first step is deciding you want to feel better.

You are only feeling bad because your mind is running in a negative thought pattern. Are you able to shut down the program? Are you able to put the computer of your mind to sleep so it can rest? If so, push the power button and wait patiently for your mind to re-boot. When it starts back up, it will be back in its innate positive thought loop.

If you are not able to force-quit the software, there is still hope. You can train your mind to switch tasks.

Which loop would you like your mind to run? How does this new program feel emotionally and physically while it is being processed?

In the moment that you take the time to imagine a new path for the mind, that path is created. The program is now open, and you can switch to it anytime you please. If you notice yourself fucking around in that old, bad-feeling software again, don't worry. You can easily switch back to the most recent version at anytime.

Soon that pesky old version will become completely obsolete.

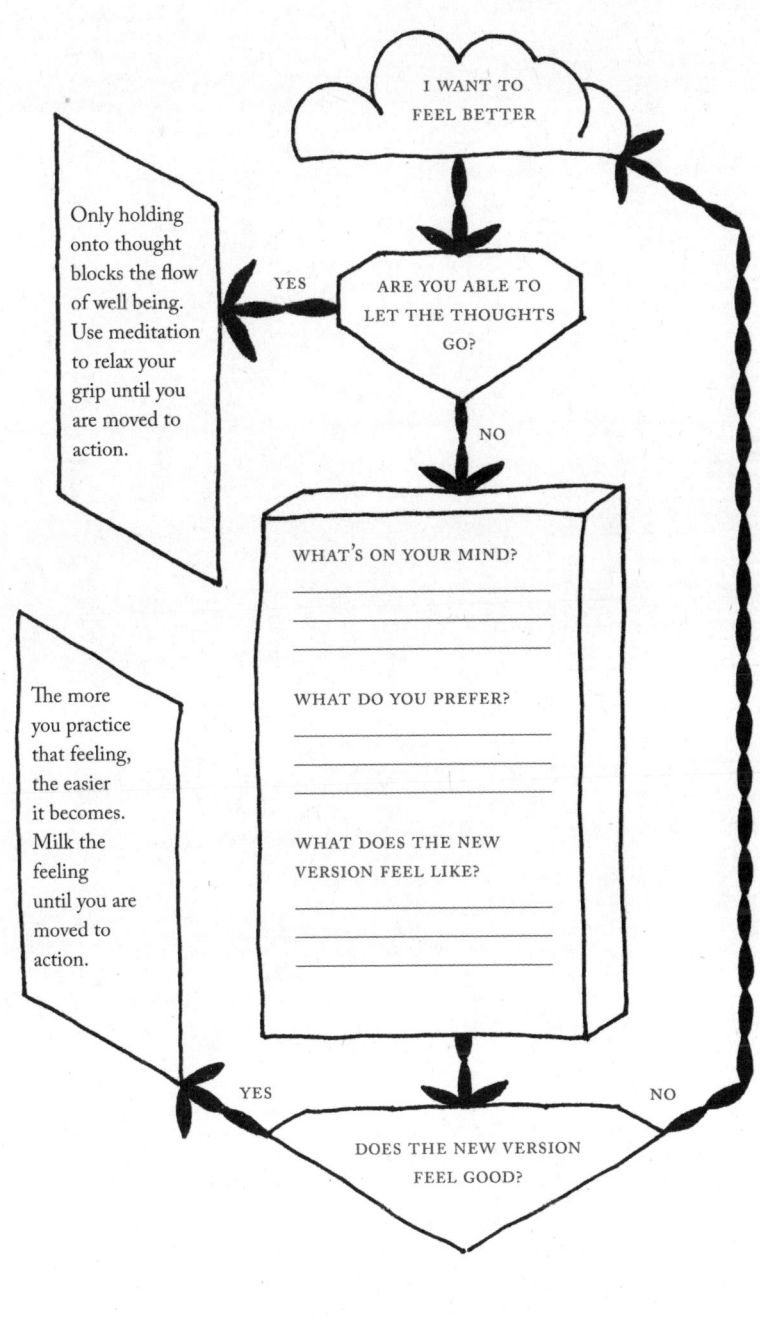

1. Date
2. Dreams
3. Today's theme
4. To do not give a fuck about
5. Intentions
6. Today's mantra/affirmation
7. I want to feel
8. Best parts of my day
9. Make a wish
10. Tomorrow I will wake up feeling

Self-love

Diets never work. Beauty products are not sustainable. The only deciding factor in whether or not you feel good about yourself is you. You'll never be skinny or young-looking enough if that is what you are looking for to be happy. But when you decide to love yourself now, suddenly, you're just as attractive as you could ever be.

Use the self-love snail on the next page to focus on the things you like about yourself. You'll notice that once your inner dialogue about yourself changes, your lived experience changes as well.

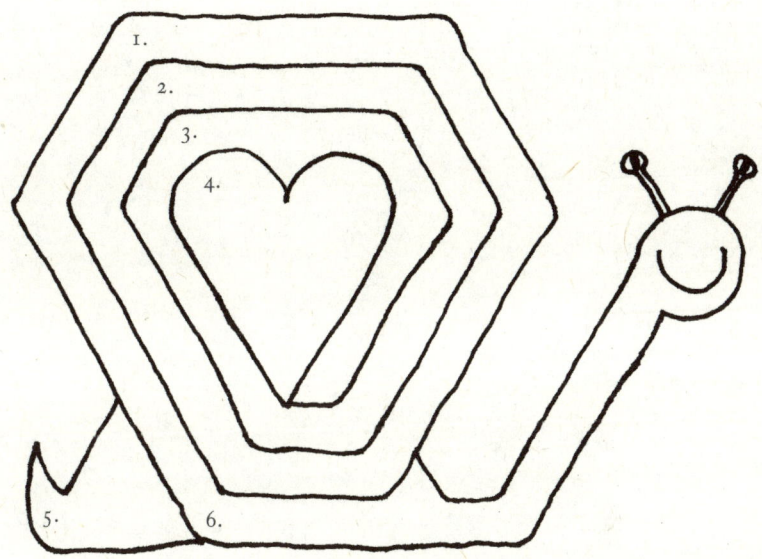

1. My best quality
2. I'm glad I did this today
3. I feel good when
4. I love
5. I thank my body for
6. I am awesome because

1. Date
2. Dreams
3. Today's theme
4. To ~~do~~ not give a fuck about
5. Intentions
6. Today's mantra/affirmation
7. I want to feel
8. Best parts of my day
9. Make a wish
10. Tomorrow I will wake up feeling

I Am

You are how you perceive yourself. This worksheet helps you choose the version of yourself you want to project. For each prompt, fill in words or images that best describe how you want to feel. For example, "I am": what or who do you want to be? "I am loved"? "I am already successful"? "I am at peace with what is"?

When you focus on who you want to be, that's who you become. You are the creator of you.

1. I am
2. I love
3. My best quality
4. A favor to do for myself
5. An act of kindness
6. A compliment to myself
7. I feel successful when
8. A dream
9. Dream bigger
10. What's working
11. One step I can take now

1. Date
2. Dreams
3. Today's theme
4. To do not give a fuck about
5. Intentions
6. Today's mantra/affirmation
7. I want to feel
8. Best parts of my day
9. Make a wish
10. Tomorrow I will wake up feeling

Life Story

One of the best ways to see what you want in physical reality is to be able to imagine it in your mind's eye. Travel to the future and tell us how your story magickally unfolded just as you foretold. Write the answers to numbers 1-4 in the space provided on the next page.

~

This is the story of how:

_____

1. What was the first indicator the magick was working?

2. Once you began gathering momentum, what evidence did you see that your dream was picking up steam?

3. Everything came together perfectly. Even more perfectly than you ever imagined. As you basked in your manifestation, what was the icing on the cake?

4. How did it feel to get everything you wanted?
Fill in your emotional reaction in the flag at the top.
Choose from the list below or write your own.

Joy	Love	Happiness
Euphoria	Exhilaration	Belief
Flow	Knowing	Optimism
Inspiration	Passion	Hope
Appreciation	Excitement	Contentment
Empowerment	Enthusiasm	Relief
Freedom	Eagerness	Confidence

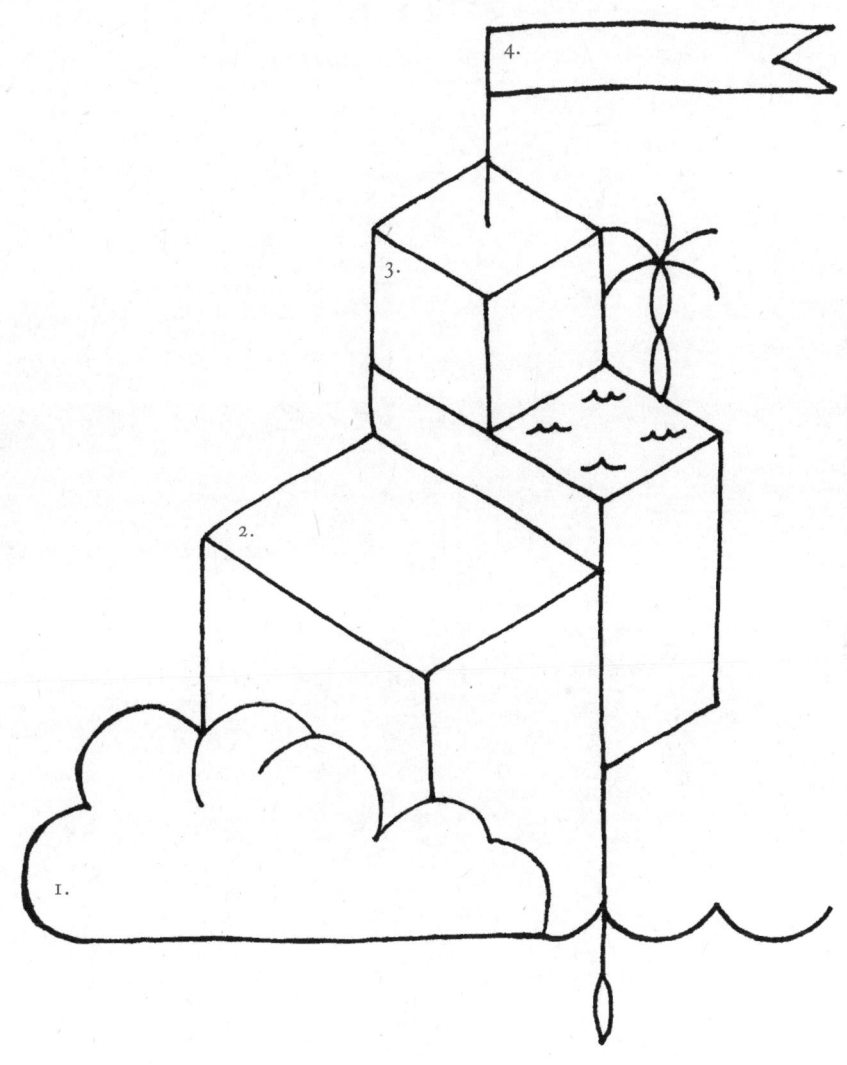

1. Date
2. Dreams
3. Today's theme
4. To ~~do~~ not give a fuck about
5. Intentions
6. Today's mantra/affirmation
7. I want to feel
8. Best parts of my day
9. Make a wish
10. Tomorrow I will wake up feeling

21

Contrast Is a Gift

In design, when we speak of contrast, we're referring to the juxaposition of light and dark that imbues a design with depth. Life design requires contrast too, for if your life was all one tone, you'd be bored to pieces with its flatness. Contrast in life is the necessary dark that makes us know light. We can't have one without the other.

Contrast is your friend. While at times contrast's tough love can be frustrating, it is always on your side. When contrast throws you for a loop, remember that it is always helping you get what you want by making you ask.

Use the space on the next page to answer the questions below. When you take the time to align with what the universe is helping you ask for, you'll realize it's already on its way.

1. What is your contrast?

2. What is the contrast helping you ask for?

Become it, then see it. Affirm. Look for evidence of what you're asking for. Attention creates. You have the choice to resist your contrast or celebrate what it's helping you create. The one you pay attention to is the one you see more of.

3. I am

4. I have

5. I love it when

1. Date
2. Dreams
3. Today's theme
4. To do not give a fuck about
5. Intentions
6. Today's mantra/affirmation
7. I want to feel
8. Best parts of my day
9. Make a wish
10. Tomorrow I will wake up feeling

22

How May I Serve

Ask yourself, "How may I serve?" then write down the first thing that comes to mind. When you serve your reality, your reality serves you.

1. Date
2. Dreams
3. Today's theme
4. To do not give a fuck about
5. Intentions
6. Today's mantra/affirmation
7. I want to feel
8. Best parts of my day
9. Make a wish
10. Tomorrow I will wake up feeling

⟨23⟩ Prepaving

Prepaving is the practice of consciously creating events before they occur. Remembering that we have control over how events unfold can turn nervousness, anxiety, uncertainty, or fear into excitement and empowerment. Envision the version you want, and celebrate your creation with the knowing feeling of everything going your way.

Before your next meeting, date, or adventure, take a few seconds to think about what you do want instead of what you don't want. Use the spaces provided on the next page to outline your vision.

1. Event title
2. What happens before the event?
3. What's the best that could happen during?
4. How do you want to feel after?

1. Date
2. Dreams
3. Today's theme
4. To ~~do~~ not give a fuck about
5. Intentions
6. Today's mantra/affirmation
7. I want to feel
8. Best parts of my day
9. Make a wish
10. Tomorrow I will wake up feeling

… 24 …

Flawless Victory

Sometimes everything just works out. You set out on an adventure or to complete a task and everything ends up going your way. After a particularly invigorating success, reflect on what helped you unlock this achievement. What worked, and how can you apply those skills to future life encounters? When you milk the feeling of your victory, you are focusing on how you like to feel, which increases the likelihood of more victories.

Warrior Name:

_____

Opponent Name:

_____

1. How did you prepare for the battle?

2. What were your special moves?

3. What fatality did you use?

4. How did you feel after your victory?

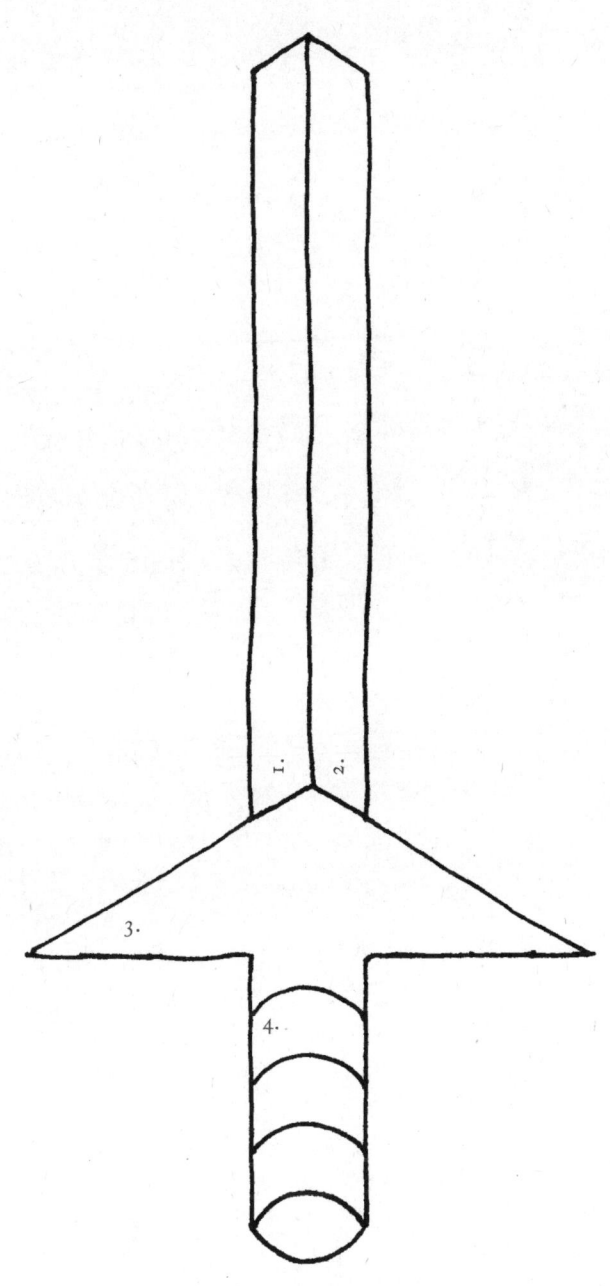

1. Date
2. Dreams
3. Today's theme
4. To do not give a fuck about
5. Intentions
6. Today's mantra/affirmation
7. I want to feel
8. Best parts of my day
9. Make a wish
10. Tomorrow I will wake up feeling

⟨25⟩
Self-doubt Alchemy

This alchemic experiment encourages you to take advantage of your resistant, fearful inner dialogue by accessing the other side of the wave and turning self-doubt into empowering and exciting affirmations of inherent truths. Every resistant thought is an opportunity to focus on and allow the feeling of its opposite. This exercise helps you release persistent negative thoughts and replace them with empowering ones.

Use the prompts on the next page to transmute your fear-based self-doubt into creative gold.

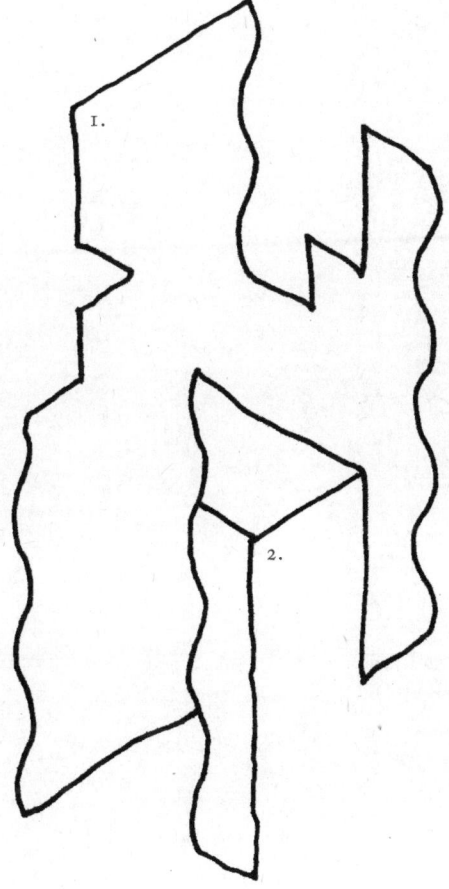

1. What I am afraid of
2. What I know to be true

1. Date
2. Dreams
3. Today's theme
4. To ~~do~~ not give a fuck about
5. Intentions
6. Today's mantra/affirmation
7. I want to feel
8. Best parts of my day
9. Make a wish
10. Tomorrow I will wake up feeling

The Cauldron

Manifestation can be as easy as a command and a flick of the wand. Other times, though, it requires multiple ingredients, some time to steep, and a little stir now and again.

Today, instead of putting all the pressure on yourself to create something, throw all the ingredients in a pot and let the magick do the rest.

Write the purpose of the spell in the space provided, then start raiding the metaphysical pantry. When measuring, consider the following:

What are you going to need on your side?
What indicators will let you know the spell is working?
What do you already have working in your favor?

Now that you've combined all the elements, you can relax knowing that they are coalescing to create a serendipitous chemical reaction that is out of your control.

A good spell takes time to simmer. Don't let your disbelief or impatience cause it to scorch. Fill in the rhyme below using the purpose of your spell and the essences you added as inspiration. When you see evidence of your spell working, or when you start to doubt it, say the chant below and know that the universe is doing its work.

_____ and _____ give me power,
Time to make my _____ **flower.**

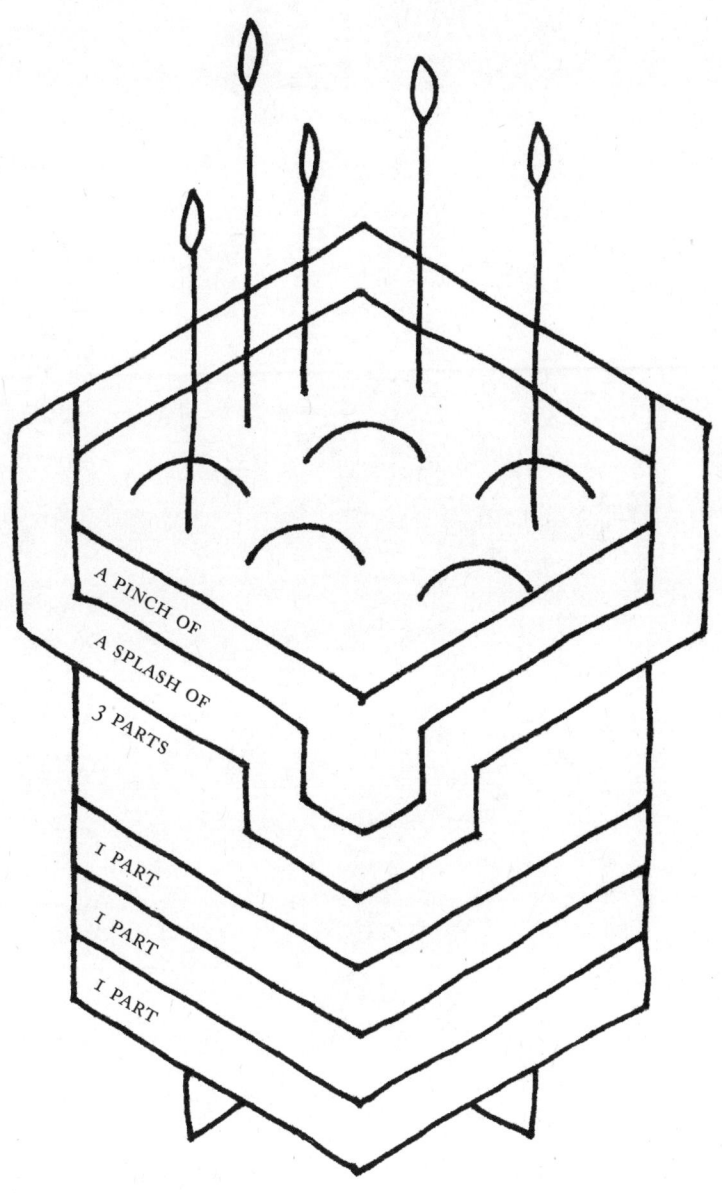

The purpose of this spell:

_____

1. Date
2. Dreams
3. Today's theme
4. To do not give a fuck about
5. Intentions
6. Today's mantra/affirmation
7. I want to feel
8. Best parts of my day
9. Make a wish
10. Tomorrow I will wake up feeling

Give What You Want to Get

When you want something from someone else, or even from life itself, you have to first become a vibrational match to it. You simply cannot attract generosity, love, affection, abundance, or anything of the like if you are not in a place to receive it. If all you can see and feel is the opposite, life's lavishness will never be apparent to you, even if it is right in front of your face.

For this exercise, think about what you want, but imagine yourself giving it. When you give what you want to receive, you become the energy of it. When you give love, you feel love, without ever having to *receive* it.

In the space provided, write down who or what you want to give something to. It could be a person, or it could be an event like "Sister's Wedding," or you could just be giving to life itself. Remember, this is really something you want for yourself, but you're going to trick your mind into already having it by giving it away.

Write down what it is you want to give and how it feels when you give it in the space provided. Really focus on the feeling of giving it and how it feels in your body.

Use all three gemstones for extra practice!

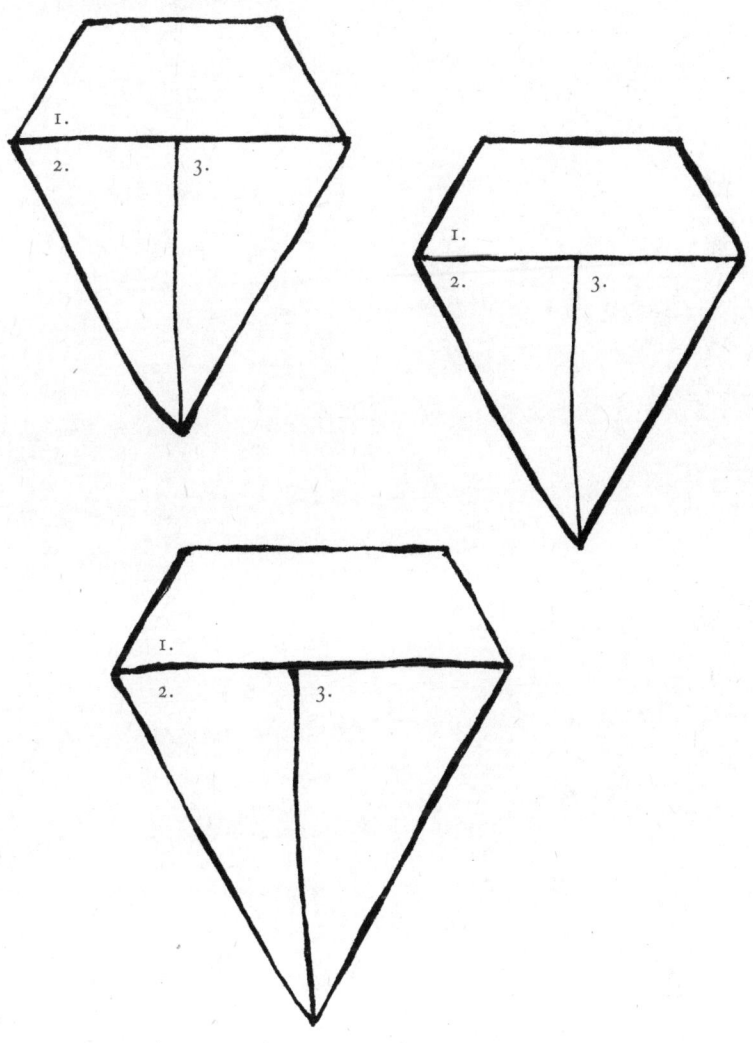

1. To whom/what do I want to give?
2. What would I like to give?
3. How will giving it make me feel?

1. Date
2. Dreams
3. Today's theme
4. To ~~do~~ not give a fuck about
5. Intentions
6. Today's mantra/affirmation
7. I want to feel
8. Best parts of my day
9. Make a wish
10. Tomorrow I will wake up feeling

⟨28⟩
Two Wings to Fly

"God turns you from one feeling to another and teaches by means of opposites, so that you will have two wings to fly, not one."
RUMI

What if there was only one side of the wave? It wouldn't be a wave. It would be a flat line. What is life as a flat line? Death.

When you are in your moment of contrast, ask yourself, "What is this causing me to ask for?" Then celebrate! Without the problem, how could you attract the solution?

Write your problem in the left wing of the angel at the right. Then write your solution in the right wing.

Notice how she couldn't fly without both?

Let your contrast be your boost. How is your problem giving you a leg up? In what way is what you don't want helping you ask for you what you do want?

1. I must experience [something bad]
2. in order to experience [something good].

1. Date
2. Dreams
3. Today's theme
4. To ~~do~~ not give a fuck about
5. Intentions
6. Today's mantra/affirmation
7. I want to feel
8. Best parts of my day
9. Make a wish
10. Tomorrow I will wake up feeling

(29)

Your Own Medicine

In each of the numbered potions on the right, write a piece of advice that you've heard yourself give someone else.

If your reality reflects you, and everything in your reality is a reflection of the signal you send, then the same is true for the people with whom you share this co-creative experience. Each person in your reality can only reflect your current beliefs about your reality.

When you hear yourself giving advice, remember it is only yourself you are talking to. Think someone could change the way she is living her life? The way you see her situation is only a reflection of your beliefs. You are noticing your own perceived short-comings.

Listen to what you are telling others to do and remember that you are only your higher self talking to reflections of yourself.

Then, take your own advice.

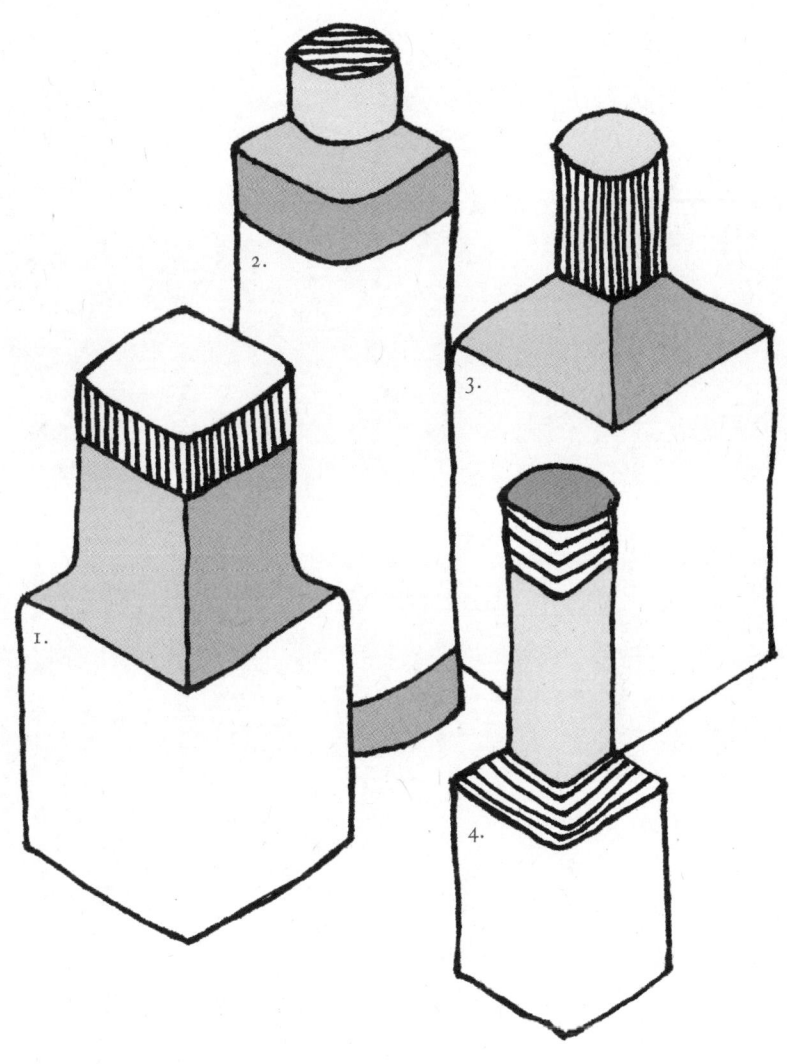

1. Friend   2. Colleague   3. Society   4. Family Member

1. Date
2. Dreams
3. Today's theme
4. To ~~do~~ not give a fuck about
5. Intentions
6. Today's mantra/affirmation
7. I want to feel
8. Best parts of my day
9. Make a wish
10. Tomorrow I will wake up feeling

Ask the Universe Anything

Go ahead, ask.

Do you believe the universe provides? Do you believe the answer is always right there winking at you, waiting for you to pay her some attention?

Of course you do. Not only do you believe, you know.

Ask the Universe Anything then trace the labyrinth while you listen for the answer.

Question:

_____

Trace the labyrinth back out while you allow yourself to take its advice.

Answer:

_____

1. Date
2. Dreams
3. Today's theme
4. To do not give a fuck about
5. Intentions
6. Today's mantra/affirmation
7. I want to feel
8. Best parts of my day
9. Make a wish
10. Tomorrow I will wake up feeling

Plant the Seed

When we experience a particularly emotional chapter in our lives—good or bad, long or short—the tendency of the mind is to replay the event over and over, either trying to resolve a conflict or mining the past for good feelings. Whether you're reliving a positive or negative experience, you are not in the now. You are looking for something outside of this now to make you feel good.

When we are able to stop thinking and be present in the now, we open ourselves up to the best of what we are able to receive. When we stop trying to solve problems or re-create romantic dates, we allow solutions and more dates to flow naturally. When we continue to run things over in our minds, we block the flow of well being and prevent the universe from doing its work.

Name your experience: _____

1. What was the best part of the experience, or what is one thing you can learn or take away from it? Write it in the space to the right.

2. Turn this flower you plucked into a present tense affirmation such as, "I let the flow do it," or, "I love it when we get along," or "I feel prosperous." Write the affirmation below the flower. This is your seed.

Now let your seed grow. When you plant something in your garden, you don't turn around the next day and dig it up; you give it time to grow. Give your seed time to grow into more flowers like the one you chose. Any time your mind tries to revisit this story, say your affirmation to yourself and picture your seed growing. Every time you drop a thought about the past and relax into the now, you nourish your seed.

1.

2. _____

_____

_____

Glossary of Terms

Flow: Named by Mihály Csíkszentmihályi, flow is a word to describe the feeling of being totally absorbed by an activity in a pleasurable and focused way. When one experiences the flow state, thoughts subside and motions become automatic, guided by the subconscious or infinite intelligence.

Magick: We spell the word magic with a "k" in this book to differentiate between stage magic and divine magick. Magick is the power to shift perspective, choose our thoughts, and therefore create a new reality. Magick is a way to describe our innate ability to co-create with the flow of life.

Synchronicity: A synchronicity is a meaningful coincidence. It is a wink from the universe letting you know you're on the right path. When life hands you the exact amount of money you need, or you run into someone you were just thinking about, know that life is encouraging you and helping you towards your goal.

About the Publisher

MICROCOSM PUBLISHING is Portland's most diversified publishing house and distributor with a focus on the colorful, authentic, and empowering. Our books and zines have put your power in your hands since 1996, equipping readers to make positive changes in their lives and in the world around them. Microcosm emphasizes skill-building, showing hidden histories, and fostering creativity through challenging conventional publishing wisdom with books and bookettes about DIY skills, food, bicycling, gender, self-care, and social justice. What was once a distro and record label started by Joe Biel in a drafty bedroom was determined to be *Publisher's Weekly's* fastest growing publisher of 2022 and has become among the oldest independent publishing houses in Portland, OR and Cleveland, OH. We are a politically moderate, centrist publisher in a world that has inched to the right for the past 80 years.

Global labor conditions are bad, and our roots in industrial Cleveland in the 70s and 80s made us appreciate the need to treat workers right. Therefore, our books are MADE IN THE USA

Did you know that you can buy our books directly from us at sliding scale rates? Support a small, independent publisher and pay less than Amazon's price at **www.Microcosm.Pub**

MORE BY SCHOOL OF LIFE DESIGN AT WWW.MICROCOSM.PUB

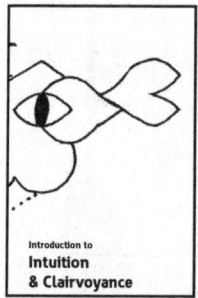
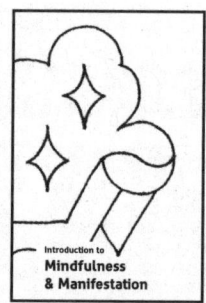

MONTHLY MAGICKAL RECORD

A 31-DAY SPELL JOURNAL
FOR MODERN WITCHES

www.Microcosm.Pub/SoLD

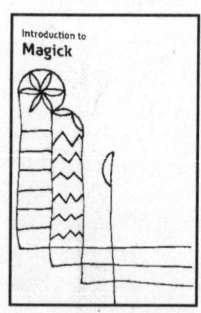

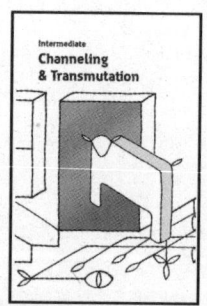

MORE EXPLORATION OF SELF AT WWW.MICROCOSM.PUB

SUBSCRIBE!

For as little as $15/month, you can support a small, independent publisher and get every book that we publish—delivered to your doorstep!

www.Microcosm.Pub/BFF

UNLOCK YOUR GREATEST SELF AT WWW.MICROCOSM.PUB

   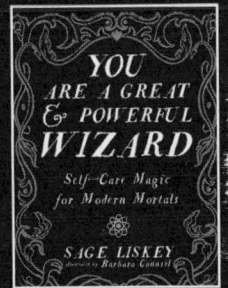

What is School of Life Design?

School of Life Design (SoLD) is a curriculum for recognizing present moment awareness, training attention and undoing social conditioning. Combining the principles of design with elements of magick, meditation, and manifestation, SoLD makes interactive guides for harnessing the creative power of thought and emotion.

Founded in 2010 by Kelly Cree and Jessica Mullen, SoLD utilizes the principles of design as a framework for shaping life experience. **Gratitude** is the use of *emphasis*: focus on what you like and what you want more of. **Mental codes** (or mantras) create peaceful mental *rhythm*. **Consciousness** is the *balance* of doing, thinking, feeling and being. **Intention** is the purposeful *movement* of energy. **Visualization** generates new *patterns* of thought and expectation. **Transmutation** creates joy out of the *contrast* of pain. **Channeling** reveals the *unity* and connectedness of all things.

When used deliberately, these tools enable you to create and experience the reality you prefer. In each moment, you are faced with a design decision: where do you focus your awareness? With daily practice of SoLD's ever-evolving methodology for lucid living, you will experience the manifestations, synchronicities and miracles you desire. Design your reality instead of the other way around; only you are the creator of you.

Learn more at
www.schooloflifedesign.com